For Emma,

Best wishes

to a

real dinosaur

expert,

'Dino'

Dan

Lessem

On a hot morning 90 million summers ago, the sunlight begins to filter down through a forest of towering evergreens in South America. The ground rumbles as huge dinosaurs plod by, pausing to tear branches off the trees. They are plant-eating dinosaurs, or herbivores, and they travel in groups, sheltering their youngsters in the center of the herd. Some of these giants, which measure five stories tall, bend their long necks to the ground to graze on ferns and bushes. Slowly, they make their way toward the muddy shore of a lake to drink.

As they are gulping the water, a bellowing roar and the crash of footsteps frighten them, causing them to flee. Suddenly, an enormous predator appears, as large as a truck, flashing sharp teeth in its gaping jaws. It charges at the youngest in the pack. Avoiding its victim's huge, swishing tail, the attacker lunges at the herbivore's neck. The bloody battle is over quickly, and the meat-eater begins to feast on its enormous prey.

It's just another day in South America, near the end of dinosaur time, and another meal for *Giganotosaurus* (JI-gah-NO-tuh-SAW-russ), "the giant lizard of the south"—the largest predator ever known to have walked the Earth.

BIGGER THAN T. REX

The Discovery of *Giganotosaurus*: The Biggest Meat-Eating Dinosaur Ever Found

BY DON LESSEM

Illustrated by Robert F. Walters

Scientific Adviser: Professor Rodolfo Coria,
Museo Carmen Funes, Plaza Huincul,
Neuquén Province, Argentina

CROWN PUBLISHERS, INC., NEW YORK

INTRODUCTION

TYRANNOSAURUS REX. Even the name is scary: the tyrant lizard king.

Sixty-five million years ago, *T. rex* was the largest, most terrifying creature alive. Weighing seven tons or more, it was heavier and longer than a school bus. Measuring at least forty feet from head to tail, *T. rex* had jaws that were longer than a fifth grader is tall. Its banana-size teeth could rip off 500 pounds of meat, as much as *eight* fifth graders, in a single bite.

From the time that the first *T. rex* skeleton was found nearly a century ago, paleontologists have called it the largest meat-eating dinosaur ever to live. Recent discoveries about how *T. rex* lived have reinforced the notion that the "tyrant lizard king" truly lived up to its name.

For example, tooth marks of *T. rex* on the bones of duckbilled and horned dinosaurs show how its bite could penetrate flesh and dig grooves in solid bone. A *T. rex* found with broken and re-healed limb bones shows that it could survive serious and painful injury. A broken *T. rex* tooth found embedded in another *T. rex*'s cheek bone shows that it would even bite the face of another *T. rex*.

For nearly a century, paleontologists had also searched for clues about what may have been even bigger killer dinosaurs than *T. rex*. But none of the fossil fragments found had led them to a recognizable species.

Several bones of one giant predator, *Spinosaurus*, were found in North Africa but were destroyed by bombs in World War II. More recently, two fossils had scientists intrigued: a skull from a huge carnivore found in North Africa and a leg bone from a super-giant found in India. In 1993, however, the search for the largest predatory dinosaur took a new turn, when scientists in Argentina found a giant carnivore—a killer dinosaur—even bigger than *T. rex!*

(left) *T. rex*: the former King of the Dinosaurs.

(bottom) The skull of *T. rex*, which grew to more than five feet in length and housed teeth eight inches long.

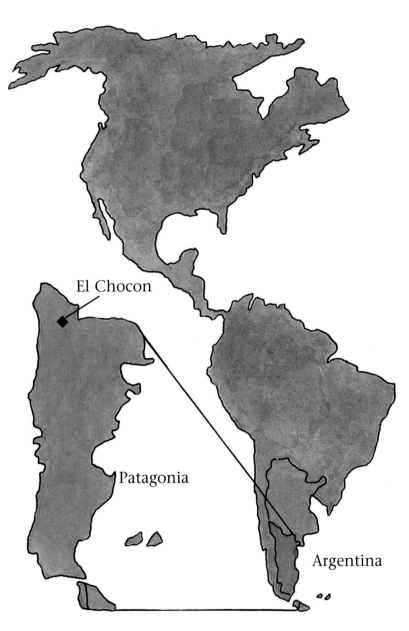

El Chocon

Patagonia

Argentina

ONE MORNING IN 1993, a middle-aged man on a dune buggy was riding across the rolling badlands of central Argentina, ten miles outside his hometown of El Chocon, in the north of Patagonia. Patagonia is a region of mountains and barren semi-desert stretching all the way to the southern tip of South America. But in the north, in the area of El Chocon, Patagonia consists of mostly dry, windswept badlands. This area, with its exposed rock nearly 100 million years old, dates back to the middle of the last dinosaur period, the Cretaceous. Inside these 100-million-year-old rocks are the bones of giant dinosaurs.

The man in the dune buggy was one of the few people who look for dinosaurs in Patagonia, an amateur fossil hunter named Ruben Carolini. On several occasions he has found the large bones of plant-eating dinosaurs in this area.

On this particular morning, Mr. Carolini spotted a big bone sticking out from the side of a hill. Thinking he'd found the thigh bone of another large plant-eater, Mr. Carolini called two paleontologists and asked them to come and examine the fossil. They were Professor Rodolfo Coria, a dinosaur paleontologist from the nearby city of Plaza Huincul, and his colleague Professor Leonardo Salgado, from the University of Comahue.

The badlands of El Chocon, where *Giganotosaurus* was discovered.

The discoverer of *Giganotosaurus*, Ruben Carolini (*center*), with professors Leonardo Salgado (*left*) and
Rodolfo Coria (*right*). Carolini is holding part of the jaw of *Giganotosaurus*.

Professor Coria's crew excavates a thigh bone (*above*) and the spinal column (*right*) of *Giganotosaurus*.

When they arrived, Professors Coria and Salgado saw the tip of the bone protruding from the soft mudstone and immediately began digging it out using their hands and a shovel. Like Mr. Carolini, the two paleontologists assumed the bone was a thigh bone of a large plant-eater, the sort of bone that is commonly found in this region. But they soon saw that the bone was not shaped like a plant-eater's thigh bone at all. It had a huge crest in the knee area, a feature found only on the shin bones of big meat-eating dinosaurs. It became clear that this bone was, in fact, a shin bone—one that belonged to a *very* large meat-eater.

Excitedly, they dug at the soft rock around the shin bone and soon found more of the giant's hind legs. Then the pelvis emerged, and finally a curved tail, with its tiny tail bones still lined up as they had been in life.

They kept digging, working without a break in the cold, windy winter. They were hoping to find the skull bones—the bones that would tell the most about the giant's identity. But skull bones are fragile, and often the many pieces are washed far away from the rest of the skeleton by the same streams that have covered and preserved the larger bones.

Yet, to the scientists' excitement and

Professor Coria (*left*), casting expert Mary Odano (*center*), and Professor Coria's crew behind the cast bones and actual fossils of *Giganotosaurus*.

surprise, they soon found the prize they sought—pieces of the dinosaur's skull.

First they uncovered the braincase—the bone that held the carnivore's softball-size brain. Then they came upon a hunk of jaw, with four of its thick, serrated teeth still intact. They spent days at the site, digging up as much of the dinosaur as they could find.

After several weeks of searching and digging, Professors Coria and Salgado and their assistants completed the excavation of the giant animal. By the end, they had dug a pit nearly twenty feet deep, thirty feet wide, and thirty feet long, and they had found what they estimated to be about seventy percent of the dinosaur.

A portion of the lower jaw of *Giganotosaurus* reveals its enormous teeth.

(above) The museum in Plaza Huincul where Professor Coria worked when *Giganotosaurus* was discovered.
(left) Excavating *Giganotosaurus* and preparing the individual bones to be moved.

THE SCIENTISTS USED little picks and brushes to clean most of the crumbly brown mudstone away from the fossils while they were still in the ground. Then they prepared the bones to be moved to the museum, using the same method scientists have used for more than a century. First they cleared away most of the dirt around the fossil, leaving the bone lying on a platform of rock. Then they soaked strips of burlap in plaster and water, and wrapped the exposed side of each fossil with the mixture. They then flipped each bone over and wrapped the rest of it. When dry, the "jacketed" fossil was lifted onto Professor Coria's truck and transported to his museum, Carmen Funes, in Plaza Huincul.

At the museum, Professor Coria carefully cleaned off the remainder of the mudstone from the fossils, using dentist's tools and tiny drills. It took nearly a year to clean the approximately one hundred individual bones that had been discovered. Now Professor Coria was ready to examine the fossils and to try and figure out just what sort of animal he had found.

(top) Casting expert Mary Odano (*left*) and Professor Coria's crew prepare *Giganotosaurus*'s skull bones for molding and casting.

(left) Sculptor Maria del Carmen Gravino creates the missing teeth for a restoration of *Giganotosaurus*'s skull.

(bottom) With small tools, Professor Coria cleans the skull bones of *Giganotosaurus* while they are still in their plaster jacket.

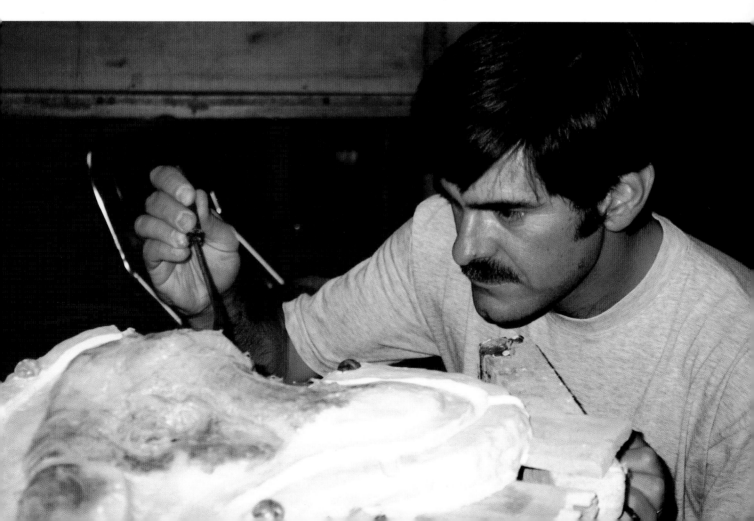

The ANALYSIS

The author (*left*) and Professor Coria examine a vertebra of *Argentinosaurus*.

LONG BEFORE HE HAD FINISHED preparing the dinosaur's bones for examination, Professor Coria knew he had found a dinosaur unlike any known in South America—or anywhere. Indeed, he and Professor Salgado had realized from the moment they began digging that they had come upon a new species of meat-eater—bigger than any ever found on their continent.

For Professor Coria it was not the first strange and amazing dinosaur he had ever found. Though he had been interested in dinosaurs as a child, he was equally interested in all things about the past, from pyramids to mummies, and in living animals as well. In college and after, he focused on paleontology and worked in Buenos Aires, Argentina's capital city, for the country's chief dinosaur paleontologist, Professor José Bonaparte. With Professor Bonaparte, Professor Coria excavated an oddly short-armed and horned twenty-seven-foot-long meat-eater named *Carnotaurus*, as well as several plant-eaters—from tiny babies to adults as big as houses.

But what was this new dinosaur? Professors Coria and Salgado were puzzled. At the dig site, the scientists pulled

The skeleton of the peculiar horned meat-eater *Carnotaurus* from Argentina.

out the dinosaur anatomy books they had brought with them. But their books were no help.

Except for *T. rex*, there was no dinosaur with a shin bone the size of the one they had uncovered. And besides, *T. rex* was known to have lived only in North America and had been found in rocks that were 25 million years younger than these. Professors Coria and Salgado began to suspect that they had unearthed perhaps the biggest dinosaur of them all.

To find out for sure, they decided to do some research: reading as much as they could about the discoveries of other giant predatory dinosaurs and visiting museums all around the world to compare their bones with the bones of other giant meat-eating dinosaurs.

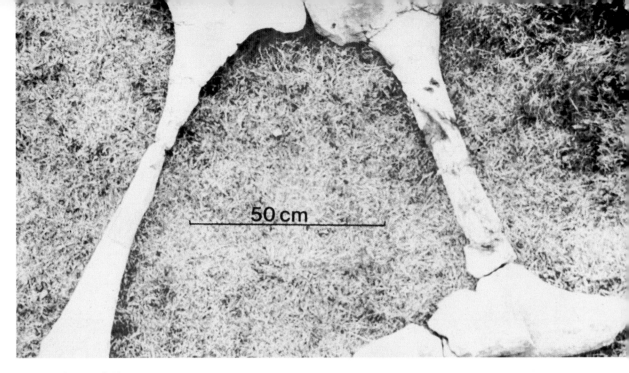

Some hip bones of *Giganotosaurus*.

To compare their bones with those of *T. rex*, Professors Coria and Salgado took photographs and made drawings, and brought them to the American Museum of Natural History in New York City. There, the comparisons they made would help them learn more about how the newfound dinosaur had evolved and what its closest relatives might have been.

They consulted with other dinosaur experts, like Dr. Philip Currie of the Royal Tyrrell Museum of Palaeontology in Canada, the world authority on meat-eating dinosaurs, who came to Plaza Huincul to see the bones firsthand. When he saw them, Dr. Currie agreed that, indeed, the dinosaur was huge—even larger in many proportions than *T. rex*—and he agreed with the conclusions Professor Coria was forming about what the dinosaur had looked like, what dinosaurs it was closely related to, and what habitat it had lived in.

Dr. Philip Currie, an expert on meat-eating dinosaurs.

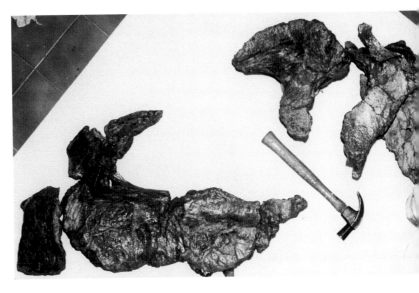

Skull bones of *Giganotosaurus*.

T. rex and fossil friends at the American Museum of Natural History in New York City.

GIGANOTOSAURUS

ALLOSAURUS

ABELISAURUS

SINERAPTOR

CARNOTAURUS

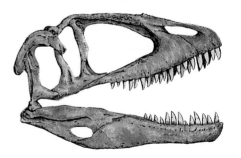

CARCHARODONTOSAURUS

1 foot

On the left: three skulls show the similarities between *Giganotosaurus* and other large South American predators from the Cretaceous Period, *Abelisaurus* and *Carnotaurus*. On the right: *Allosaurus*, the largest North American predator of the Late Jurassic, had a smaller but more powerful jaw than *Carnotaurus*. *Giganotosaurus*'s skull is also similar to that of *Sineraptor*, from China, and *Carcharodontosaurus*, from Africa.

GIGANOTOSAURUS

CAREFUL STUDY OF THE BONES of the giant predator revealed it had a uniquely long skull, narrow shoulders, and large hind limbs and vertebrae. When the skull bones were reassembled, they showed that the dinosaur's head was about five feet six inches long—nearly twice the size of the heads of large predators previously known from South America, such as *Abelisaurus* and *Carnotaurus*. The skull was even six inches longer than the head of the largest known *T. rex*. But was the body larger?

It was difficult to compare *Giganotosaurus*'s size to *T. rex*'s. Although its shoulders were smaller than those of *T. rex*, the most accurate comparison would come from comparing the bones most often used to estimate an animal's length, the femurs (also called thigh bones). When both were measured, the results were impressive. The femur of "Sue," the largest *T. rex* ever found, measured about four feet six inches (1.38 meters), while the new predator's femur was four feet eight inches (1.43 meters)—two inches longer. And it was thicker. Professors Coria and Salgado were excited! The newly discovered dinosaur was probably the largest meat-eater yet known.

Studying several other meat-eaters helped Professors Coria and Salgado make some conclusions about where *Giganotosaurus* might have fit into the evolution of giant predators throughout dinosaur time.

Comparison to the newfound skull of the giant carnivore from North Africa, *Carcharodontosaurus*, showed that the two meat-eaters shared a very long and narrow lower jaw and thin teeth. By comparing fossils, they could tell that both came from the same time period—nearly 100 million years ago. This suggests that South America and North Africa may have been one big continent at that time.

Giganotosaurus also had features in common with *Carnotaurus*, a dinosaur that belonged to a family of large South American meat-eaters called abelisaurs. This suggests that *Giganotosaurus* may have been an ancestor of the abelisaurs.

But where exactly did *Giganotosaurus* itself come from? Of all the earlier giant dinosaurs, *Giganotosaurus*'s head appears to most closely resemble the skull of *Sineraptor*, a large meat-eater that lived in China more than 150 million years ago. *Sineraptor* was not the direct ancestor of *Giganotosaurus*, but the similarity in the shape of its skull suggests that perhaps *Giganotosaurus* descended from dinosaurs that have been found in Asia. Perhaps these dinosaurs roamed all over the world when the Earth was still a single continent in the Jurassic Period. Or perhaps the land in China, South America, and North Africa was linked during the Cretaceous Period in ways that scientists have not yet discovered.

One hundred million years ago, South America was dominated by giant *araucarian* conifer trees, giant plant-eating dinosaurs

And what was the country like when *Giganotosaurus* roamed across it? According to Professors Coria and Salgado, the soft mudstone indicates that this predator was buried where it lived, in an ancient floodplain of lakes and slow-flowing streams.

The rock was slightly older than the harder, pebbly sandstone that contained the fossil of the largest plant-eater, *Argentinosaurus*. That dinosaur had been buried in a swift-flowing stream that was powerful enough to scatter even its enormous bones, mixing them with large rocks and stones.

But the bones of other giant plant-eaters were found in the same area as the new giant predator. The scattered bones appear to belong to at least two different kinds of giant four-legged herbivores. One was *Andesaurus*, a dinosaur more than forty feet long. The other was a whip-tailed giant, at least as large as *Andesaurus*, that is still unnamed.

Plant fossils have yet to be found in the area. But it is likely that there were forests, and an environment far warmer and wetter

such as *Rebbachisaurus (left)* and *Andesaurus (center)*. On the right is the giant predatory dinosaur *Giganotosaurus*.

than the Patagonian badlands of today. The dominant tree was probably a huge conifer with oddly fanned leaves. A tree like it called the monkey puzzle tree survives today in the Southern Hemisphere. But all through dinosaur time, these *araucarian* trees were among the biggest, especially in the southern continents.

So if the professors' conclusions are right, *Giganotosaurus* was a heavy predator lumbering among even larger and heavier plant-eaters in a rich and well-watered warm forest. Why did all these dinosaurs grow to be so huge? Perhaps the lush environment of their time favored the growth of such super-giant dinosaurs.

This is but one of the many mysteries about *Giganotosaurus* that Professor Coria is trying to answer. Will he eventually find more bones of this giant and be able to get an even better idea of its appearance? Will he learn more about its environment and the other animals it lived with? And will he find clues to its behavior in the form of footprints or other fossils?

While many questions still awaited answers in 1995—two years after they began their excavation—Professors Coria and Salgado were ready to officially describe their find based on all their detailed measurements and comparisons. In a paper written for a scientific journal, they explained exactly how they knew that what they had found was an undiscovered species of new dinosaur. And they gave it its official name.

Choosing a name wasn't easy. A scientist who makes the first published scientific description of a dinosaur can name the dinosaur after anything at all. Usually, scientists will use Greek or Latin terms to describe a key feature of the dinosaur or to record the place where it was found. For example, *Seismosaurus* is the longest dinosaur ever found (it was more than 125 feet long), and its name means "earthquake lizard." And *Argentinosaurus*, which measured 100 feet long and weighed 100 tons, was excavated by Professor Coria, who named it after his native country.

Professors Coria and Salgado felt "like parents struggling to find a name for their unborn child," as Professor Coria recalls. They joked about naming the dinosaur *"Kick-butt-tyrannus."* They liked the name *Gigantosaurus*, "giant lizard," but a large plant-eating dinosaur had been given that

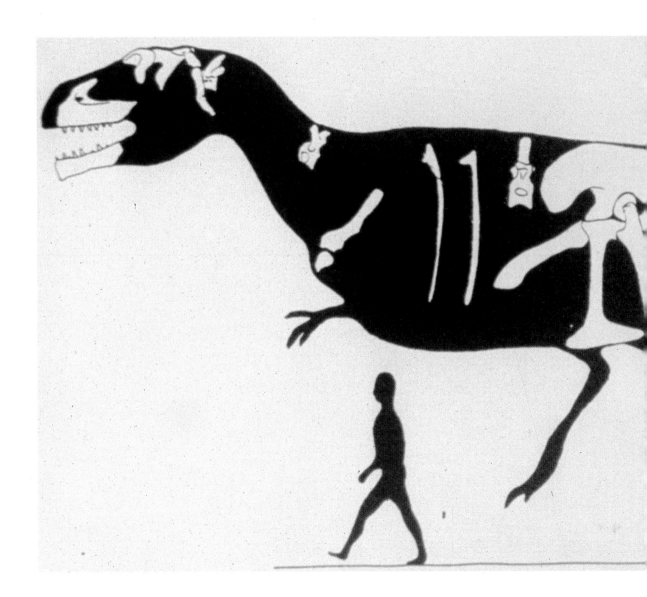

name long ago. So they chose a name very close in spelling but different in meaning—*Giganotosaurus*—(HEE-gah-NO-tuh-SOUR-russ, as pronounced in Spanish)—"the giant lizard of the south." For a species name, they chose *carolinii,* in honor of Ruben Carolini, who discovered its first bones.

Giganotosaurus carolinii became an officially recognized new dinosaur when Professors Coria and Salgado submitted their description along with photographs and drawings of the fossils to one of the most famous of all scientific journals, *Nature.*

When the article finally appeared in *Nature* in September of 1995, reporters all over the world began calling Professor Coria at all hours of the day and night to learn about the new king of the killer dinosaurs. For two weeks, Professor Coria did nothing but answer questions about the new discovery.

Suddenly, he and his little city, as well as the dinosaur he had named, became famous around the world. He and Professor Salgado were even awarded a medal of honor from the Argentine National Senate. Professor Coria was overwhelmed. "I cannot believe it. It seems funny to me. I dig dinosaurs all my life, and suddenly everyone wants to know about it."

So it goes when you find the biggest carnivore that ever stood on the Earth.

This diagram, comparing the size of a human to *Giganotosaurus,* appeared in several of the articles announcing the discovery.

EPILOGUE

FAREWELL, *T. REX*. A new king lives. Long live *Giganotosaurus!* But how long will *Giganotosaurus* reign? Perhaps not very long. A new kind of dinosaur is found on average every six weeks.

Chances are that somewhere in the world there was once an even larger dinosaur predator. And, besides, scientists cannot be sure exactly how big *Giganotosaurus*, *T. rex*, or any of the other giant dinosaurs actually grew. With only one or, at best, a few specimens of each, they simply can't be sure of the full size range of these animals. If you met only a dozen people, none of them a huge basketball player, would you know that humans could grow to over seven and a half feet tall?

There will be many other giant dinosaurs discovered in the future. For now, however, there is a new champion among predators: *Giganotosaurus*, the biggest meat-eating dinosaur of all.

The earliest dinosaurs lived about 228 million years ago, in the Late Triassic Period. They were probably meat-eaters and were no bigger than dogs. Gradually they grew to much larger sizes. The first meat-eater known to top twenty feet in length was *Dilophosaurus,* the twin-crested carnivore inaccurately portrayed as the cute little poison-spitter in the movie *Jurassic Park.*

All meat-eating dinosaurs shared several basic features throughout their evolution. For instance, they all had S-shaped necks; they all had four toes on each foot, with the first toe a very short one; they all ran on their hind legs; and they all had hollow bones and other features similar to their descendants, birds. Some were toothless, but most had powerful jaws with sharp, notched teeth.

Over the 163 million years of dinosaur evolution, there were many kinds of meat-eaters, known as *theropods,* ranging from the size of chickens to as long as trucks. Despite their varying sizes, their overall body design changed little. "They are no more different than different models of Ford automobiles," says paleontologist Philip Currie.

Yet the biggest meat-eating dinosaurs did grow bigger, with more powerful jaws, lighter skeletons, and fewer fingers. The first meat-eaters had five fingers. The last, such as *T. rex*, had only two.

MEAT-EATERS

THE FIRST KILLER GIANT EVER FOUND

MEGALOSAURUS
Pronunciation: MEG-uh-luh-SAW-russ
Meaning of name: "big lizard"
Family: Megalosauridae
Size: 23 to 26 feet (7 to 8 meters) long
Fossils found: England, France, Portugal, China, Utah
Period: Middle Jurassic, 175 million to 155 million years ago

©1996 Bob Walters

Megalosaurus was the first meat-eating dinosaur ever discovered. Half of its big lower jaw, with large, curved, sharp teeth still in place, was discovered in a stone quarry in Oxfordshire in the south of England early in the nineteenth century. *Megalosaurus* was named in 1824 by Sir William Buckland, a famous and eccentric British scientist whose hobby was feasting on freshly killed zoo animals. Professor Buckland knew from the sharp, serrated teeth on the lower jaw that the animal was a large and heavily built meat-eater long gone from the Earth. In addition to the jaw, only a few back bones, parts of the hips, and back legs were found.

It was not the earliest large carnivorous dinosaur, but it was probably the largest of its time, about 165 million years ago.

THE STRANGE REPTILE

©1996 Walters

ALLOSAURUS
Pronunciation: AL-uh-SAW-russ
Meaning of name: "strange lizard"
Family: Allosauridae
Size: 30 to 40 feet (9 to 12 meters) long
Fossils found: Colorado, Wyoming, Utah,
   Montana, Tanzania, Australia
Period: Late Jurassic, 156 million to 145 million
   years ago (in North America)

From fossil evidence, the best known by far of all the large meat-eating dinosaurs is *Allosaurus*. It was an enormous animal, heavily built like the smaller and earlier meat-eater *Megalosaurus*. *Allosaurus* had massive legs, a huge tail, and a thick, short body and neck, even compared with other giant meat-eaters. All of its weight—more than two tons—rested on two feet with four widely spread toes: three facing forward and a shorter one pointing backward. Its front limbs were short but powerful, with three sharp-clawed fingers on each hand.

The true killing weapons of *Allosaurus* were its spectacular jaws. Its head grew to a length of more than three feet, and its thick teeth—pointed, curved, and notched—could crush bone or slice meat. For a few decades, in the late 1800s, *Allosaurus* held the distinction of being the largest meat-eater of all. Its bones were first discovered in Colorado in 1869.

In 1927, a treasure trove of *Allosaurus* bones was found in central Utah, at a site known as the Cleveland-Lloyd Quarry. The allosaurs found there ranged in size from youngsters just ten feet long to adults more than thirty-nine feet long. In the jumble of bones, a possible allosaur egg was found, indicating that this site may have been a nesting colony and nursery for young allosaurs.

THE MISSING SAIL-BACKED DINOSAUR

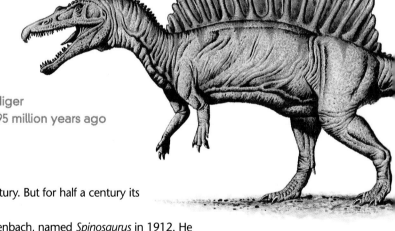

SPINOSAURUS
Pronunciation: SPY-nuh-SAW-russ
Meaning of name: "spine reptile"
Family: Spinosauridae
Size: Up to 49 feet (15 meters) long
Fossils found: Egypt, Tunisia, Morocco, Niger
Period: Late Cretaceous, 97.5 million to 95 million years ago

Spinosaurus has been famous for nearly a century. But for half a century its fossils have been missing.

A German paleontologist, Ernst von Reichenbach, named *Spinosaurus* in 1912. He identified this giant meat-eater from jaw, neck, back, leg, rib, and tail bones found by German prospectors at an oasis in Egypt. The bones were shipped to Germany, and all were destroyed by bombing raids during World War II.

Spinosaurus's teeth were long but thinner, smoother, and more cone-shaped than the teeth of other meat-eating giants. Its skull was long and low, more like a crocodile's than like the heads of most giant carnivorous dinosaurs. Some scientists have suggested that *Spinosaurus* ate mainly fish, snagging them with its long jaws and teeth.

The high-spiked back bones showed the distinctive sail—which rose up to five and a half feet—on the back of this animal. If these dinosaurs were not fully warm-blooded, their sails might have been energy-saving devices. Like a car radiator, the sail may have helped warm the dinosaur in the morning and cool it at midday, for it lived in a hot and moist region near the equator.

Since only bits of pieces of *Spinosaurus* have ever been discovered, and those have been missing for decades, it is difficult to estimate just how big this dinosaur was. But its back bones measured over seven inches long, a full inch longer than those of *T. rex*. While not nearly as heavy as *T. rex*, *Spinosaurus* could well have been longer—perhaps nearly fifty feet in length!

THE KING IS DEAD

TYRANNOSAURUS REX
Pronunciation: tye-RAN-uh-SAW-russ recks
Meaning of name: "tyrant lizard king"
Family: Tyrannosauridae
Size: Up to 45 feet (14 meters) long
Fossils found: Montana, Wyoming, South Dakota,
    North Dakota, New Mexico, Colorado,
    Alberta and Saskatchewan, Canada
Period: Late Cretaceous, 74 million to 65 million years ago

©1996 Walters

T. rex was the last and biggest of the tyrannosaurs, the final group of large dinosaur meat-eaters. Among the tyrannosaur family's special features were small two-fingered hands and especially large and powerfully built skulls with huge, curved teeth. T. rex's teeth were the largest of any dinosaur's. They grew to a length of eight inches and were nearly an inch thick—sharp enough to slice through thick hide and strong enough to smash through bone.

The bones of T. rex were first uncovered in the early 1900s by scientists from New York City's American Museum of Natural History. For more than half a century, only three partial T. rex skeletons were known. Some parts of the animal, including its arms, had never been seen. Artists and sculptors incorrectly imagined it as a three-fingered beast that stood upright. Decades of illustrations of this dinosaur standing upright furthered the myth of a tail-dragging T. rex. Twelve feet of fake tail were added to make it stand tall in its display at the American Museum of Natural History.

During the past decade, more than a dozen partial skeletons of T. rex have been found, making it now one of the best understood of all dinosaurs. Two nearly complete skeletons were found in 1990, one in Montana and the other in South Dakota. Both showed T. rex's previously unknown two-clawed hands and stumpy arms. Its arms were so short its hands could not even touch each other. They may have had no practical use at all.

The skeletons also show that T. rex was a long-legged animal, built to run faster than earlier giant predators. Its senses—hearing, smell, and sight—were probably keen; and for a dinosaur, its brain was large. T. rex has proved far more frightening than scientists and artists originally imagined.

SAUROPHAGANAX
Pronunciation: SAW-roh-FAY-guh-NACKS
Meaning of name: "king of the reptile eaters"
Family: Allosauridae
Size: Up to 49 feet (15 meters) long
Fossils found: Oklahoma
Period: Late Jurassic, 145 million years ago

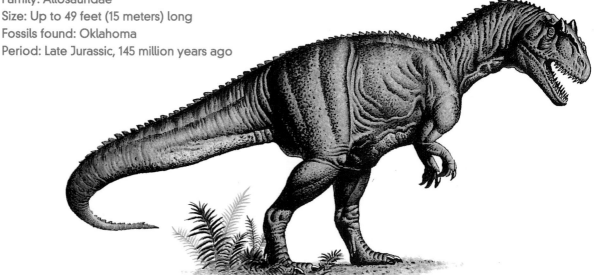

©1996 Walters

Another allosaur-like predator from the Late Jurassic was excavated in Oklahoma in the 1930s. Its fossils are now being studied for the first time. Its original name, *Saurophagus* ("lizard eater"), was changed to *Saurophaganax* ("king of the reptile eaters").

ACROCANTHOSAURUS
Pronunciation: ACK-roh-KAN-thuh-SAW-russ
Meaning of name: "high-spine lizard"
Family: Allosauridae
Size: Up to 45 feet (14 meters) long
Fossils found: Oklahoma, Texas
Period: Early Cretaceous, 115 million to
    105 million years ago

©1996 Walters

Acrocanthosaurus was also a spine-backed giant meat-eater, but it lived many millions of years before *Spinosaurus*, and in a different part of the world: the American Midwest. The spines on *Acrocanthosaurus* were about two feet tall and encased in thick tissue, unlike the tall, narrow spines of *Spinosaurus*. Despite having spines in common with *Spinosaurus*, *Acrocanthosaurus* looked more like *Allosaurus*.

For years, *Acrocanthosaurus* was thought to be an animal about thirty feet in length. But in the early 1990s, prospectors in Oklahoma discovered an *Acrocanthosaurus* skeleton more than forty feet long. This little-known predator may have grown as large as the biggest *T. rex*.

THE LONG-ARMED MYSTERY

DEINOCHEIRUS
Pronunciation: DYE-noh-KYE-russ
Meaning of name: "terrible hand"
Family: Unknown
Size: Large (measurements unknown)
Fossils found: Mongolia
Period: Late Cretaceous, 80 million
   to 65 million years ago

©1996 Walters

Which was the strangest, most mysterious meat-eater of all? The winner is *Deinocheirus*, hands down. In fact, that's all we have of the "terrible hand"—a pair of front limbs more than eight feet long! Each long arm ended in three clawed fingers.

Discovered by Polish women scientists in Mongolia, and identified in 1970, the arms were unusually huge for a meat-eating dinosaur. As big as these arms were, though, they may not have been such frightening weapons, since they were lightly built. The claws were broad, on fingers that were not especially flexible.

Some researchers have speculated that they are the claws of a huge ostrich-like ornithomimid dinosaur. Ornithomimids were meat-eating dinosaurs known to have grown to twenty feet in length, with especially long legs that made them the fastest of all dinosaurs. Ornithomimids could not have been fierce predators, however, since they had few or no teeth at all! Instead, they may have trapped small mammals and insects with their long, nimble arms and horny beaks.

Was *Deinocheirus* a super-giant ornithomimid? Some scientists think so. Others suggest it may have been a dinosaur that behaved like the modern sloth, a slow-moving animal with giant arms that climbed trees.

If the rest of its body was proportioned like other giant meat-eating dinosaurs, *Deinocheirus* might have been the largest meat-eater of all.

Recently, paleontologist Dale Russell has speculated that it may have been a segnosaur—a strange and little understood Mongolian dinosaur that walked on all fours.

Perhaps paleontologists will someday solve the mysteries of *Deinocheirus* and determine just how enormous and strange it really was.

THE INDIAN SUPER-GIANT

BRUHATHKAYOSAURUS
Pronunciation: BREW-hath-KAY-oh-SAW-russ
Meaning of name: "huge body lizard"
Family: Unknown
Size: Up to 65 feet (20 meters) long
Fossils found: India
Period: Late Cretaceous, 74 million to 65 million years ago

Try to imagine a meat-eating dinosaur twice as heavy and twenty feet longer than *T. rex*.

That is what two Indian scientists reported in 1989 when they found enormous dinosaur leg bones near a village in southern India. One bone was a hip bone, the ilium, and it was the same size as that of a *T. rex*.

But along with the ilium they found a lower leg bone more than six and a half feet long and nearly three feet thick at each end. The size of this bone and a fragment of a thigh bone suggest an animal far larger than *T. rex*. When the scientists estimated the dinosaur's size, they realized it must have been enormous, so they named it *Bruhathkayosaurus*, "huge body lizard." It may have weighed fifteen tons and measured sixty-five feet long! As one researcher wrote of its incredible size: This dinosaur "makes *Tyrannosaurus rex* look like a chicken."

But there is a good chance that *Bruhathkayosaurus* was not a meat-eater at all. Other scientists, who have not seen the bones, are puzzled by these measurements. How could such enormous leg bones fit together with a hip bone the size of *T. rex's*?

These researchers suggest that the Indian scientists may have discovered the remains of two *different* animals: a giant meat-eater, perhaps as large as *T. rex*, and a giant plant-eater. Plant-eating dinosaurs grew to three times the length of *T. rex* and many times its weight.

A GIANT REDISCOVERED

CARCHARODONTOSAURUS
Pronunciation: kahr-CHAR-uh-DON-tuh-SAW-russ
Meaning of name: "shark lizard"
Family: Unknown
Size: Up to 45 feet (14 meters) long or more
Fossils found: Morocco, Algeria, Egypt
Period: Early Cretaceous, 113 million to
    90 million years ago

As was the case with *Spinosaurus*, *Carcharodontosaurus*'s bones were destroyed in bombing raids during World War II. But in the spring of 1995, paleontologist Paul Sereno of the University of Chicago was climbing a remote and rocky slope in southern Morocco when he found much of the skull of an enormous meat-eater.

The giant's teeth were identical to those known to have come from the missing *Carcharodontosaurus*, but considerably larger. To Dr. Sereno's amazement, these teeth belonged in a skull as long as, or longer than, the head of *T. rex*—at least five feet in length.

Dr. Sereno announced his new find in the spring of 1996. He hopes to return to Morocco again to look for more of the animal, though his crew found only a skull on its first search.

Carcharodontosaurus may be closely related to *Giganotosaurus* of South America, and could have lived during a similar time. Both these giant meat-eaters had narrow teeth for slicing meat and thin, long lower jaws, whereas *T. rex* and other tyrannosaurs had thick teeth and more powerful jaws for crunching bone.

Several of the animals described in this book are new or little-known discoveries that have only been described in scientific papers. At this time, *Giganotosaurus* is mentioned in only two other popular books, *Dinotopia: The World Beneath* by James Gurney and *Dinosaur Worlds* by Don Lessem.

Here are some references that provide additional information about the meat-eating dinosaurs as well as information on related subjects:

BOOKS:

The Dinosaur Society Encyclopedia by Don Lessem and Donald F. Glut (Random House). A comprehensive encyclopedia of all dinosaurs, including many recent discoveries.

Dinosaur Worlds by Don Lessem (Boyds Mill Press). Details all dinosaurs through time along with their environments, including plants and insects. *Giganotosaurus* is featured.

The Complete T. Rex by Don Lessem and John R. Horner (Simon & Schuster). One scientist's view of the life and times of the former king of the dinosaurs. For older children and adults. Heavily illustrated.

The Illustrated Dinosaur Encyclopedia by Dr. David Norman (Crescent Books). Written by a leading dinosaur paleontologist, this is the best review of dinosaur evolution for any age group. Beautifully illustrated by John Sibbick.

The Macmillan Illustrated Encyclopedia of Dinosaurs and Prehistoric Mammals by Dougal Dixon, Barry Cox, R.J.G. Savage, & Brian Gardiner (Macmillan). A good overview, well illustrated, with brief entries.

Dinosaurs by Dougal Dixon (Boyds Mill Press). A child-friendly, well-illustrated overview.

The Golden Guide to Dinosaurs by Eugene Gaffney (Golden Books). A small, brief, and useful reference book.

The Dinosaur Data Book (Avon). A good reference book with brief descriptions of many dinosaurs.

VIDEO:

Dinosaurs. The four-hour PBS series, now available on video (WHYY-Philadelphia).

T. rex Exposed. The excavation and popularization of *T. rex,* from the PBS NOVA series (WGBH-Boston).

MULTIMEDIA:

Microsoft Dinosaurs (Microsoft). Selected dinosaurs, video, and guided tours.

Dinosaur Adventure (Knowledge Adventure). A dinosaur game with some information. For younger children.

Don Lessem has been on dinosaur digs in Argentina, Mongolia, the Arctic, and numerous other places around the world; he has reported on paleontology and other science topics for the *Boston Globe,* the *New York Times, Life,* and other publications. His books for adults include *Dinosaurs Rediscovered,* a survey of dinosaur discoveries around the world. His more than fifteen books on natural history for children include *Inside the Amazing Amazon,* a fold-out book about the Amazon rain forest; *The Iceman,* about the discovery of a 5,300-year-old man; and *Digging Up Tyrannosaurus Rex,* with John R. Horner, about the unearthing of the first complete *T. rex* skeleton ever found. Mr. Lessem is the founder of the Dinosaur Society, a nonprofit organization created to promote dinosaur science, and is a consultant for dinosaur movies and theme parks, including the film *Jurassic Park* and theme parks for Universal Studios. He lives in Waban, Massachusetts, with his wife and two daughters.

To Heda Kovaly: an explorer of the heart
    —D. L.

Text copyright © 1997 by Don Lessem
Illustrations copyright © 1997 by Robert F. Walters

Photographic credits: Page: 7, 10 (*top right*), 15 (*top left*): Don Lessem; 8, 9, 10 (except *top right*), 11 (*top right*), 14, 15 (*top*), 20-21: Rodolfo Coria; 11: (*top left , bottom*): Mary Odano; 12: Ignacio Salas-Humara; 13: Professor Jose Bonaparte, Museo de Ciencias Naturales, Buenes Aires; 15 (*bottom*): American Museum of Natural History, © Scott Frances.

Published by Crown Publishers, Inc., a Random House company, 201 East 50th Street, New York, New York 10022

CROWN is a trademark of Crown Publishers, Inc.

Printed in Hong Kong
http://www.randomhouse.com/

Library of Congress Cataloging-in-Publication Data
Lessem, Don
Bigger Than T. Rex: the discovery of the biggest meat-eating dinosaur ever found by Don Lessem; illustrated by Robert F. Walters; scientific adviser, Rodolfo Coria.
p.   cm.
Includes index.
Summary: Describes the discovery and reconstruction, in Patagonia, of the fossil remains of the largest carnivorous dinosaur yet known.
1. Giganotosaurus carolinii — Juvenile literature.
[1. Giganotosaurus carolinii. 2. Dinosaurs. 3. Paleontology. 4. Fossils.]
I. Walters, Robert F., ill. II. Title.
QE862.S3L445   1997
567.97 — dc20
96-30562

ISBN 0-517-70930-9 (trade)
ISBN 0-517-70931-7 (lib. bdg.)

1 0 9 8 7 6 5 4 3 2
First Edition